FROST FAIRS ON

THE FROZEN THAMES

By Nicholas Reed

The Thames Frost Fair of 1684   *Guildhall Library, Corporation of London*

Published by
Lilburne Press
1 Dover House
Maple Road
London SE20 8EN
Tel: 020 8659 5776

First Edition 2002

ISBN 1 901167 09 7

When and Why did the Thames Freeze?

In London, the Thames froze solid at least 23 times, between 1309 and the last time in 1814. But never again. Why not?

One possible reason might be if the temperature did not reach the low level it attained during the Fairs. During the last two Frost Fairs, the average temperature in 1739-40 (December to February) was 31 degrees Fahrenheit, and in 1813-4 was 32.5 degrees. But in our coldest recent winter, that of 1962-3, the average temperature was 31.5 degrees, yet the Thames showed no sign of freezing anywhere near London.

The reason for its freezing cannot be due to the temperature alone: there must have been other reasons.

An artist's reconstruction of "shooting the rapids" under the old London Bridge.

All the Frost Fairs took place upstream from the Old London Bridge. When London Bridge was built in stone in 1209, it had 19 arches. (By contrast, the modern London Bridge has only three.) In addition, each of the 20 piers had a "starling" round it: a breakwater which protected each pier from the force of the water and any debris which might damage the pier. These breakwaters diminished the flow of the water through the arches even more than the piers themselves, so the bridge structure acted almost like a dam against the flow of the water. This meant that for much of the time, if one wanted to travel along the river, one had to "shoot the rapids" at London Bridge, being pushed very fast by the current through the Bridge. Indeed by the 18th century the starlings took five sixths of the width of the river, leaving only a small part of the river width for the entire flow of the Thames. Little wonder the drop in waterlevel between the two sides of the bridge could be as much as six feet.

Under the arches, debris could quickly get stuck and block the flow even more, so the river above the bridge would usually be calmer and flow more slowly than below it. The slower the river flowed, the more likely it was to freeze. If the debris blocking the flow included chunks of ice in winter, the effect would be more marked, and freeze-ups even more likely.

The strongest evidence that it was the presence of the Old London Bridge which caused the Thames to freeze, is shown by what happened when that bridge was replaced. In 1831 the new bridge with just five arches, designed by John Rennie, was opened, and the old bridge removed. After that time, there were no further frost fairs on the Thames. In 1895, in southern England, the temperature dropped to 30 degrees below freezing. Despite that, the Thames, though it carried large ice floes, did not freeze across anywhere in the London area, but only far upriver. The Frost Fairs were no more.

A view of London Bridge in 1600, showing the large breakwaters or "starlings" around each pier of the bridge, which impeded the flow of the River. (In the foreground is Southwark Cathedral.)

The first references to the Thames freezing over are from the 12th century, and the first occasion when some kind of fair took place was in 1309. Of this, we are told that there were sports, dancing, a bonfire, and a hare hunted. The five occasions when it froze most extensively, and the Frost Fairs which resulted, are well recorded in contemporary paintings and prints, from 1683, 1715, 1739 and 1789, with the last such Fair in 1814. But before looking at them, let us examine the first clear representation we have of the frozen Thames.

THE FROZEN THAMES IN 1677

This is a painting, now in the Museum of London, by Abraham Hondius, a Dutchman, completed in 1677. Hondius was living in London at this time, and the large size of the painting, some six feet in width, much larger than most contemporary paintings, has suggested it was commissioned from him. If so, the man shown prominently in the middle, throwing a snowball, may be the one who commissioned it. Be that as it may, the pictorial evidence the painting gives us has never been closely examined.

We are looking downriver toward the old London Bridge, with its many houses perched on it. On the far right in the distance is Southwark Cathedral, and further left from that, the top of the tower of St.Olave's Church in Tooley Street.

In the foreground are at least six large icebergs, each with several thin sheets of ice on the top. The level of the river can be seen several feet below their tops, and ice has also formed on this lower surface. The icebergs, even allowing for artistic licence, seem to be at least six feet thick. The suggestion that they were composed of close packed snow seems highly unlikely: would snow on the river be six feet thick? Rather, it is more likely the Thames froze to a depth of six feet at or near this point. As the tide rose, the ice layer would have broken up, causing the gaps we see in it. As the tide went out, it stranded the large blocks of ice on the river bed. By the time the tide returned and surrounded the icebergs, thick ice had formed on the surface of the water. This ice was then deposited on top of the existing icebergs, leaving the thin sheets of ice we see on top. The tide has then dropped back to its lower level and frozen again, creating the surface of water and ice shown in the painting.

The Frozen Thames in 1677
Painting by Abraham Hondius,
(c. 1630-1695)
© Museum of London

Above the people on the stairs, the hanging inn sign shows a Dutch hat inside a wreath. The tavern this represents has not yet been identified, but there would have been many inns along this part of the Thames.

This was not a Frost Fair: the ice was far too rugged and dangerous to allow more than a single file of people in the middle distance following a path all the way across the ice. The only woman visible (Detail 2, top left) appears to have a tray of refreshments on her head – and is being accosted by two hungry walkers. On the left (Detail 1), people are approaching the river down the steps which would normally lead to the boats. We can see that all the men are wearing hats, apart from one on the left, who has his hand to his head.

At the far right of this detail, a gentleman is putting his hand reluctantly into his pocket. The probable reason is that, in this year, those who normally ferried people across the river, officially known as "watermen", were charging everyone a standard charge (it was sixpence in later years) to walk down on to the ice. It was only as the walkers reached the other side of the river that they found they had to pay another sixpence to get off the ice! – hence the man paying up has a rueful expression on his face.

Detail 1: At top left is a man holding his hand to his head, as he has lost his hat.
At lower right someone is holding his hat out to him.
At far right is the man putting his hand into his pocket.

Detail 2, with the man throwing a snowball in the middle.

Detail 3: showing a Dutchman on his skates. Note his Dutch hat, with a higher crown and narrower brim than the English hats opposite.

THE FROST FAIR OF 1684

In 1677 there was no Frost Fair as such. However, in 1683-4 the cold weather came back with a vengeance. Once again the river froze, and this time the Watermen were ready. A whole street of tents was created on the ice between Temple Stairs and the South Bank, on the same site as the previous freezing, upstream from London Bridge.

The Fair features in another painting by Hondius, also in the Museum of London. This shows a Thames with a much smoother surface than before, and numerous activities taking place on the ice.

Let us place the scene more accurately. We are looking northward from the South Bank, with London Bridge out of sight to the right. On the far bank, in the centre of the painting, are the buildings of the Middle Temple, one of the lawyers' Inns of Court. To the right, with the battlements and short spire, is the circular Temple Church, founded in the 12th century by the Knights Templars. In the year when this view was painted, 1684, Christopher Wren had just completed 'beautifying' the Church by adding battlements and buttresses. Also at this time, the west porch of the Church contained a music shop where Samuel Pepys used to buy copies of the latest popular songs.

In front of the Middle Temple is Temple Stairs, leading down to the river, or in this case, to the street of booths. The tall arched building on the left was called Essex Buildings, and was a major piece of property development, completed in 1680, with Essex Stairs in front: both named after the Earl of Essex, one-time favourite of Queen Elizabeth.

On the far left is the spire of St. Clement Dane's Church, now in the middle of the Strand. The Church had been rebuilt by Christopher Wren in the 1670s, but is shown before the graceful additions to the spire put on in the 1720s.

The Frost Fair of 1684,
by Abraham Hondius
© Museum of London

Incidentally, there was a scandal here in 1725. A new painting in the Church was supposed to represent St. Cecilia, the patron saint of music. It had actually been painted to portray the wife of James, the Catholic Old Pretender, following their recent marriage. When this was realised, the painting was hastily removed. The artist, however, escaped being prosecuted for treason.

Having located the position of the Frost Fair, let us look more closely at its contents. The tents for the fair were made of blankets, stretched over redundant oars provided by the watermen. (Two such oars are visible in Hondius' panting of 1684, at the end of the left-hand row of stalls.) Hence the name of Blanket Fair or Freezland Street, as it appears in some prints and engravings of the time. One of the remarkable things about these prints is that several were produced using printing presses which stood on the ice. The presses are not visible in the engravings of 1683, but one print is labelled "Printed on the Frozen Thames Feb. 1684", and the top of the "Printing Booth" can be seen in the street of booths.

By referring to contemporary prints we can see better what was going on. The activities are described in a poem which accompanied one of these engravings, so I have taken the clearest picture, and numbered the activities accordingly. The whole engraving is from a similar viewpoint to the painting. It is considered in two halves, to show the details better.

> The various sports behold here in this piece
> Which for six weeks was seen upon the ice.
> Upon the Thames the great variety
> Of plays and booths is here brought to your eye.

> 1   In blanket-booths, that sit at no ground rent
>   Much coin in beef and brandy there is spent.
> 2   Here boats do slide, where boats were wont to row.
> 3   Where ships did fail, the Sailors do them tow
>   And passengers in boats the river crossed
>   For the same price as 'twas before the frost.

The "Drum Boat" is so called in the caption because a man in the front of the boat banged a warning drum – an early predecessor of the red flag carried in front of the earliest motor cars. Horses are shown pulling various loads: how did they keep their grip on the ice? It is possible they had studs put on their shoes, as happens now. But in the past, in country areas when it was icy, it was common to wrap horses' hooves in linen cloth, which gave them a grip.

The usual cruel animal sports are shown, such as bull-baiting and bear-baiting, which were taken for granted in those days. At top right, we see a fox hunt. We do know that King Charles II joined in a fox-hunt on the ice, and frequently viewed the scene from the Palace. As this would have been Whitehall Palace, the river must have been frozen as far up as Whitehall.

A Fair of Wonders: print of 1684: right half.   Guildhall Library, Corporation of London

4   Here roasted was an Ox before the Court
        Which to much folks afforded meat and sport.
5   Three Ha'perth for a Penny, here they cry
        Of gingerbread. Come: who of it will buy?
6   The rabble here in chariots run around
7   Coffee and tea and Rum do here abound.
8   This is the printing booth, of wondrous fame
        Because that each man there did print his name
        And sure, in former ages, ne're was found
        A press to print, where men so oft were drowned.
9   A Chariot here so cunningly was made
        That it did move itself, without the aid
        Of horse or rope, by virtue of a spring
        That Vulcan did contrive, who wrought therein.
10   The Dutchmen here in nimble cutting skates
        To please the crowd, do show their tricks and feats.
11   This place the pastime us of football yields
12   At ninepins here they play, as at Moorfields.
13   The rooks at nine-holes here do flock together
        As they are wont to do in summer weather.

The carriage moved "by virtue of a spring" - a sort of clockwork car – might be very useful these days, with the shortages of petrol and calls for non-polluting transport! Vulcan was the god of fire and metal-working, hence his ability to forge a spring. But the fact this car only appears at this frost fair suggests it could not work on dry land, and relied on the slippery surface of the ice. Perhaps a spring was placed underneath the carriage, and this pushed and slid against the icy surface as it moved. The nearest equivalent would be the cotton-reel moved by two matches and a rubber band, which is familiar to many schoolchildren.

As in 1677, it was only the visiting Dutch who brought and used their skates, because they often skated on frozen canals back home. English boys and men simply slid along the ice in their shoes.

The "rooks at nine-holes" are also referred to as "pigeon-holes" in this print. They seem to have been a row of holes cut in a baulk of timber, into which one had to roll a ball, in order to score. The game survives as a fairground attraction, but normally played on tables now, with holes cut into a flat board.

In the far distance we can see "nine-pins playing". These feature in the front of Hondius' painting of 1684, and are the equivalent of skittles nowadays.

A Fair of Wonders: print of 1684: left half   Guildhall Library, Corporation of London

Perhaps the most important event at this Fair was a visit by King Charles II. This is commemorated by a card, now in the Museum of London, which was "printed by G Groom, on the Ice, on the River of Thames, January 31, 1684." At this and the later frost fairs, visitors could have their names recorded at printing presses on the ice, and this card records the presence of King Charles II and his Queen Katherine, James, Duke of York (later James II) and his wife Mary, their daughter Princess Anne (later Queen Anne) and her husband Prince George of Denmark, and finally "Hans in Kelder". This is like the expression "a bun in the oven", it refers to a "little Hans" because Anne was pregnant at the time with a German princeling, though it turned out to be a daughter, not a son. It is a remarkable, and tragic, fact, that though Queen Anne produced 17 children, only one of them survived infancy – to die at the age of 12.

CHARLES, KING.
JAMES DUKE.
KATHARINE, QUEEN.
MARY DUTCHESS.
ANN, PRINCESSE
GEORGE, PRINCE.
HANS IN KELDER.

London: Printed by G: Croom. on the ICE, on the River of Thames, January 31. 1684.

If one looks closely at the right-hand side of Hondius' painting of 1684 (Detail 1), an enormous crowd can be seen on the ice, observing what seem to be military manoeuvres. In particular, three cannon are visible, and the furthest one has just been fired. There is no record of a massacre of hundreds of innocent civilians on the Thames at this time: the cannon fire must be in tribute to someone. Perhaps this part of the painting commemorates the visit of the Royal Family, in which case the tightly packed group in the centre of the detail might be the Household Cavalry guarding them, and firing off a salute.

On the left of the painting (Detail 2) can be seen a sledge flying a flag, being pulled around in a circle by a line of six men. A similar group is visible in the engraving, where it is called "A Whirling Sledge". This is the very earliest form of roundabout: we shall see a later version in a picture of 1740.

*Details from the 1684 painting
by Hondius.*

*Detail 1, above:
Crowds surround the military
forces, with three cannon at left.*

*Detail 2, right:
In the foreground, a large sledge
is being pulled by two horses. In
the middle, six men can be seen
beside a post, pulling a sledge
around in a circle.*

John Evelyn, who kept a diary like Samuel Pepys, records that the Thames had also frozen near Westminster. He says, "At this time there was a foot-passage quite over the river, from Lambeth Stairs to the Horseferry at Westminster, and hackney coaches began to carry fares from Somerset House and the Temple to Southwark." In January 1684, the Duke of York wrote to his son-in-law William (later King William III), "The weather is so sharp and the frost so great that the river here is quite frozen over, so that for these three days past, people have gone over it in several places, and many booths are built on it between Lambeth and Westminster, where they roast meat and sell drink."

So in effect, this whole stretch of the river appears to have frozen, from Westminster right down to London Bridge. As we shall see, the same thing occurred in 1739-40.

Also in this year, James Norris in Temple Bar produced a print (opposite) which sets us several puzzles. It features a mysterious figure called "Father Erra", and the poem which accompanied the print implies he was a prophet (rather like Nostradamus). Behind this figure can be seen several of the elements we saw earlier: "a coach crossing the ice", "sliding in skates" etc., but the greater puzzle is the right hand side. There, we see a cluster of tents, a caption "The Music Booth" under them, then a single tent marked "William Bence", and under that "Three Pilgrims returning from F.H." Mr Philip Cox has spotted that F.H. might come from the prologue to Chaucer's Canterbury Tales, which refers to pilgrims returning from "ferne halves", that is, "far-off shrines". Another possibility is pilgrims returning from "fanum Hierusalem": the temple of Jerusalem. But there are no pilgrims visible in the print, and it would be a strange title for a tavern. Instead, I suspect this was the title of a song which may have been the theme tune of William Bence, if he was the musician in the Music Booth. If so, anyone who saw his name would recognise the song title. So far, Mr Bence has not been found among composers of the time, but it is more likely he was a popular musician playing anonymous popular songs.

All the prints show us a variety of taverns. This one shows "The Bottle of Hay", and next to it another with a pair of antlers on top. As a contemporary rhyme puts it.

> "Kind master, drink you beer or ale or brandy?
> Walk in, kind sir, this booth is the chief.
> We'll entertain you with a slice of beef.
> And what you please to eat or drink, 'tis here.
> No booth like mine affords such dainty cheer."

The freeze lasted from mid-December to mid-February, and the poem we quoted earlier concludes: "In six hours this great and rary show
> Of booths and past-times, all away did go."

Within the illustration the following labels appear:

Erra Pater's Prophesy or Frost Faire 168

Roasting an Ox

The Bottle of Hay

Slyding in Skeats

A Coach crossing the Ice

The Loyall Printing house

A Bull baiting

The River of

A Boate Sayling on the Ice

The Musike Booth

William Bence

Three Pilgrims returning from F.H

Thames

Erra Pater's Prophesy: a print of 1684   Guildhall Library, Corporation of London

THE FROST FAIR OF 1715

Pictures of this fair are scarce, though we know the river froze for two months, in December 1715 and January 1716. According to a later description, "As the country ice was not then stopped by a bridge at Fulham, nor that at London broken every twelve hours by the high tides, the river was passable from one side to the other, and great numbers of booths were built."

Two engravings show us what went on. The first looks down the Thames towards London Bridge, with Southwark on the right, but the buildings shown are simplified so much they are virtually unrecognisable. This time the booths look rather like Red Indian wigwams, with a tall pole in the centre of each, and the tent draped either side. In the Frost Fair shown earlier, all the booths seems to have been square, and were held up by the oars the watermen were not using. (See especially the foreground of the 1684 painting by Hondius.) There is no obvious reason for this curious change in construction, unless it was simply that so many more stalls were present from 1715 onwards, that the watermen could only provide one oar per tent. As one souvenir of 1716 says it was printed on the Thames at Westminster, this indicates that once again, the river froze all the way from Westminster to London Bridge.

The activities shown in the first print opposite are neatly listed, numbered A to N. It is worth noting there are two sorts of printing press depicted at D and H: the Printing Booth and the Rowling (rolling) Press. The first was a simple flat bed press, the latter more like an old-fashioned mangle, with two rollers squeezing the paper through. "The Geneva Booth" refers to gin being sold here (the Dutch for gin is still "Jenever"). "Huffing Jack" has not yet been explained. But as for "Will Ellis, the Poet, and his Wife Bess, Rhiming on the hard Frost", this is presumably an act rather like the 1990s TV show "Whose Line is it Anyway?", where one person presented a subject or line, and the other had to produce a poem from it. Mr Ellis seems to be holding the script, and his wife would produce the rhyme to fit it. Alternatively, perhaps she had memorised his poems and could recite the whole poem, once he gave her the first line of each.

For food for the visitors, as well as the gingerbread stall, there was also an ox, roasted by a Mr Atkins. It was a Mr Hodgson who slaughtered it, and claimed the right as an ancestral one. According to him, his father had knocked down the ox roasted on the river in the Fair of 1684, so he himself did so in 1715 and 1739. Another unusual presence at the fair was "an enthusiastic preacher, who held forth to a motley congregation, with a zeal fiery enough to have thawed himself through the ice, had it been susceptible to religious warmth."

The engraving reproduced at bottom right shows on the left some kind of dramatic or acrobatic performance taking place on a simple stage, while on the right sits a large gentleman whose deportment is very 18th century. (Though he looks like Dr Johnson, he cannot be, as Dr Johnson was only seven at the time.) The print gives us a much better idea of the elegance of the dress of some of the grander visitors to the Fair. We know that the Prince of Wales (later George II) visited, so perhaps he appears in the lower illustration.

Behold the Liquid Thames now frozen o're,
 That lately Ships of mighty Burthen bore.
The Watermen for want of Rowing-boats,
Make ufe of Booths to get their Pence and Groats.
Here you may print your Name, tho' cannot write,
'Caufe num'd with Cold ; 'tis done with great delight.
Then lay it by, that Ages yet to come,
May fee what Things upon the Ice were done.
 From the Printing-houfe in Bow Church-Yard.

Mr David Hannott

Printed on the Ice, at the
Maidenhead at Old-fwan
Stairs, Jan. 25. 1715-16.

A. The Nine-pin Playing.
B. Cripple Atkins roafting an Ox. C. Boys fliding.
D. The Printing Booth. E. The Mufick Booth.
F. A Shoulder of Mutton roafting in a String at the
  Sign of the Rat in a Cage. G. The Tavern.
H. The Rowling Prefs. I. The Geneva Booth.
K. The Gingerbread Stall. L. The Goldfmiths.
M. Huffing Jack. N. Will. Ellis, the Poet, and
his Wife Befs, Rhiming on the hard Froft.

Above: the Frost Fair of 1715-16   Guildhall Library, Corporation of London

FAIR ON THE THAMES, 1716.

THE FROST FAIR OF 1739

For the next Fair of 1739, we have a magnificent painting by Jan Griffier the Younger (c.1690-1750), grandson of the Griffier who painted our cover picture. Unusually, this is a view from near Westminster, looking down the river towards London Bridge. In the distance, we see St. Paul's, and on the far left, the twin blocks of Essex Buildings again. But the stretch of frozen river we are shown is the part downriver from Westminster Bridge. Westminster Bridge was only completed in 1750: for decades, the waterman had fought against it, as it would reduce their income from ferrying people across. They were eventually paid the magnificent total sum of £25,000 in compensation. But at this time, 1739, only two piers of the bridge had been completed, and they are visible on the right.

The river looks far more rugged and broken-up than at the previous fairs we have looked at. We do know that during this winter the ice in London was broken up every twelve hours by the high tides. One presumes that this time the flow of the river was so strong that as the tide went down, the ice floes which hit the bottom were upended by the force of the flow, and so created this rugged effect.

There were at least two paths across this section of the frozen river. Both are visible in the painting: one on the right, where Westminster Bridge was completed afterwards: the other path is roughly along the line of the later Lambeth Bridge. This one has stalls along the path at either end, but the central section just has a line of pedestrians in single file. The centre of the river where the flow of water was quickest, took longer to freeze, and thus would have been too thin to support stalls, but could support a single file of people on foot.

Even a close look at Griffier's painting does not show us much of the contents of the stalls, though a trestle table is seen on the left, with flagons standing on it. Nearby, several dogs, as well as people, are venturing onto the ice.

Opposite: Jan Griffier's the Younger's painting of the Frost Fair of 1739, in the Guildhall Art Gallery, Corporation of London.

Above is a lithograph in the Guildhall Library (Corporation of London) showing tents on the ice. People are using an ordinary ladder to climb up the left pier of Westminster Bridge, and a rope ladder to climb up the right pier. This pier must have been taller, as it was closer to the centre of the river. Hence they needed a rope ladder to climb it.

On the right, a detail from Griffier's painting, showing the two piers with people climbing up them.

More details from the Griffier painting. Above: we see people enjoying themselves
in taverns set up on the ice. Below: visitors try to skate or slide on a patch of ice.

One engraving entitled "The English Chronicle, or Frosty Calendar" was printed on the Thames in January 1740. This shows us a variety of events on the ice, and indicates that, as in the previous two fairs, there was a line of stalls leading from Temple Stairs across to the middle, but this time joining a line of stalls at right angles which led all the way down to London Bridge. Of course, the geography may be simplified, just as the buildings shown on London Bridge are extremely stylised. The stalls described include goldsmiths, turners (which must be wood turners), milliners, toyshops and a gaming table. Another stall was selling Tunbridge Ware, which is a form of decorative woodwork used normally on smaller items such as tea caddies and boxes.

In the bottom left hand corner are "flying coaches", forming a roundabout. This one is more mechanised than the primitive one of 1683, because now, four coaches are placed on top of a wheel, held by four spokes. The wheel is spun on a central pole, which itself is fixed to a gantry. The wheel with its four coaches could then, one supposes, be spun round quite easily on the ice, with an occasional push from one of the spectators.

In itself, this would only have been possible on a frozen slippery surface. But it must later have occurred to someone that, if the coaches and the wheel were raised above the ground, the wheel with its passengers could be spun even on dry land. Hence, in one form, we have the modern carousels with their prancing horses; in another form, the modern children's roundabout.

Engraving from "The English Chronicle"
Guildhall Library, Corporation of London

LONDON

Thames Street

Buttons or Buckk?

Bung your Eye

Rowling Prefs Printers. D ẙ comon Prefs Printers. E Milleners.
Flying Coaches. I Gameing Table K aBear baited. L an Ox roasted
Printed on the Thames Ian: 1739-40.

WILLIAM HOGARTH AT THE FROST FAIR OF 1739-40

William Hogarth's Portrait of himself and his dog, Trump, painted in 1745, in the Tate Gallery.

On the opposite page is another souvenir of the Frozen Thames, printed in February 1740, with a Punch and Judy show visible in the foreground.

Of the five booths shown, four of them have different sorts of printing presses inside, for printing souvenirs like this one. In the square booth on the far right, someone is putting their hands on a table with compartments. Above and leaning against it, is another such table. The level table contained the small letters for the printing press, the upper case contained the capital letters. Hence the expressions Upper Case and Lower Case letters!

Normally, the name of the visitor who bought the engraving is printed underneath. This print commemorates the visit of "Trump". He was actually the pet dog of the artist William Hogarth, and appears prominently in Hogarth's Self-Portrait now in the Tate Gallery. So the artist unselfishly decided to obtain this souvenir of his visit with his dog's name on it, rather than his own.

Scythians of Old like us remov'd,
In Tents thro' various Climes they rov'd;
We bolder, on the Frozen Wave,
To please your Fancies toil & Slave.

Here a Strange Group of Figures rise,
Sleek Beaus in Furs salute your Eyes;
Stout Soldiers shiv'ring in their Red,
Attack the Gin and Gingerbrea;

Cits with their Wives, & Lawyers Clerks,
Gamesters, & Thieves, young Girls & Sparks.
This View to Future Times shall Shew,
The Medley Scene you Visit now.

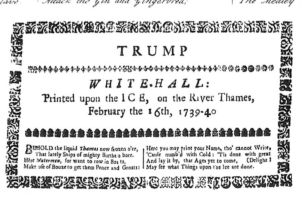

TRUMP

WHITE-HALL:
Printed upon the ICE, on the River Thames,
February the 16th, 1739-40

BEHOLD the liquid Thames now frozen o'er,
That lately Ships of mighty Burthen bore,
Here Watermen, for want to row in Boats,
Make use of Booze to get them Pence and Groats:
Here you may print your Name, tho' cannot Write,
'Cause numb'd with Cold: 'Tis done with great
And lay it by, that Ages yet to come, (Delight I
May see what Things upon the Ice are done.

THE FROST FAIR OF 1789

The most extensive of all the Frost Fairs was in 1788-9. It is tantalising that there appears to be only one picture of it.

In November 1788 the temperature in London sank to 11° below freezing, and the river stayed frozen throughout December and January. This time it froze all the way from Putney right down to Rotherhithe, a mile below London Bridge. Amusements were placed on the ice at several places: they included roundabouts, puppet-shows, bear-baiting, and a variety of wild animals on display. As before, printing presses were set up to produce souvenirs.

On the left of the engraving, under the shelter of a sail, people are drinking and dancing, with a man on the far left taking off his skates. Above him, hanging from the side of the ship which is frozen into the ice, is a cage with a cat – presumably stuffed – inside. The caption above it is "The Original Cat in the Cage, by T. Roberts". The Cat in the Cage must be the name of the makeshift tavern beside the cage, while T. Roberts is perhaps the name of the artist who produced this view.

Earlier Frost Fairs took place upstream from London Bridge, and needed the Bridge to act like a dam, so the water above it could freeze solid. This time, why did the river freeze below the Bridge? One can only assume it was the extreme cold, so much greater than before, that created the conditions for the river to freeze at Rotherhithe as well.

Up at London Bridge, there were three water-wheels which provided the power for driving water along pipes into the City. During the cold, they had to pour boiling water on the wheels to get them moving, and 25 horses were used every day to remove the ice from around the wheels.

The Thames frozen solid at Rotherhithe in 1789.
This scene was at Rotherhithe Stairs, just east of Cherry Garden Pier

THE FROST FAIR OF 1814

The last Frost Fair on the Thames lasted just one week, in February 1814, and by this time, London Bridge looked very different.

In 1756 the Bridge was so old – some 600 years old - that it looked likely to collapse if drastic action were not taken. So in that year an Act of Parliament was passed, to allow the demolition of all the houses on the bridge, and to allow the original bridge, just 20 feet wide, to be widened with a further 13 feet on each side. Canaletto must have heard about this intention, and made a pen and ink sketch (now in the British Museum) of the old bridge with its houses, just before their demolition. Once cleared of houses, the bridge was fitted with balustrades, interspersed with stone alcoves and iron light fittings. (Two of these alcoves survive in London in the grounds of Guy's Hospital, and in Victoria Park.)

It is this new widened bridge which features in the background of paintings of the last Frost Fair. This lasted just one week: from 29th January to 5th February 1814, and in area was confined to the stretch between London and Blackfriars Bridges. The most distinguished artist to visit it was the 21-year-old George Cruikshank, who produced a precociously skilful engraving, entitled "Gambols on the River Thames, February 1814."

Passengers in carriages on the bridge look down on an animated scene. On the left we read "The Thames Printing Office", with "Copper Plate Prints done in the best style by J Water Wagtail & Co." We see the printer inking a sheet, before it is placed through the rollers of the printing-machine nearby.

On either side are tented taverns called "The Nelson" and "The Shannon". Inside "The Shannon" we see a hot toddy being brewed, next to a courting couple. But the middle-aged couple behind are not in such a kindly mood: they are about to brain each other: the woman, with a bottle, and the man, with a pair of bellows. In the middle of the print, a couple are dancing a jig, to the accompaniment of a fiddler. He, however, is distracted by the sight of a woman falling heavily on the ice, grabbing the periwig of a gentleman nearby, and pulling him over as well.

In the background, clouds of smoke arise from a stall where the seller cries, "Here's my stinking hot sasengers (sausages) a penny a pint," while top left is a sign advertising "Gin and gingerbread sold here."

A lithograph by George Cruikshank, produced in 1814, when he was just 21.
Guildhall Library, Corporation of London

In the foreground on the right is a waterman, with his Doggett's race badge on his left arm, supervising the ninepins he has set up. A sailor with a pipe is taking aim at them with a wooden ball. Behind him, a man with a peg-leg has discovered with horror that the ice will only take the weight of a complete foot, not that of his wooden leg.

LA FOIRE SUR LA THAMISE

This print by Luke Clennell is entitled both "The Fair on the Thames 1814" and also "La Foire sur la Thamise", so it was aimed at French customers as well. In the centre is the 18th century equivalent of the coconut-shy: a man on the left is throwing sticks at white balls placed on iron supports on the ice, while the woman in charge smokes her pipe and holds further balls in a basket, and sticks under her arm. On the right, the old-fashioned roundabout we saw before has been replaced by the thrills and spills of two swing-boats. These were called the High Flyer and the Skylark, with each boat taking three passengers at either end. A hot toddy, like the one we saw in Cruikshank's engraving, is being brewed up in the tent at the back. On the left, a sailor with his distinctive striped shirt is dancing a hornpipe. He is accompanied by musicians playing drum, tambourine and, at far left, what must be a hurdy-gurdy, as it has a keyboard in the front and a handle at the side. Hanging high above them is the body of a sheep about to be roasted.

The Fair on the Thames 1814,
by Luke Clennell
Guildhall Library, Corporation of London

Above we see a man fastening skates to his shoes. These were long curved skates, such as were still used in the Fenlands until the last War. They were more useful for travelling long distances, than the short distances and frequent turns necessary for modern skating.

The most detailed of all the prints of 1814 was published by J Pitts of Seven Dials. In the background can be seen the City of London, with thick smoke emerging from every chimney. This may well explain the unusually thick fog, which lasted eight days and preceded the Frost Fair. Fogs preceded the other fairs, and no doubt the smog prevented any possibility of sunlight lessening the cold.

The long procession of visitors is queuing up to have their names printed by no less than three printing presses on the ice. On the right are the "Frost Fair Printing Office" (as seen already in the Cruikshank drawing) and "Letter Press Printing", while on the left is "Copper Plate Printing". The printing machine for copper-plates was much larger, because the lines were more finely drawn, and greater pressure was needed to make a clear impression on the paper. So it used a large spoked wheel like a windlass, which was turned using both arms and legs, as one can see on the left in this engraving, and in more detail on the next page. This time, London Bridge is on the right, and Blackfriars Bridge, built in 1769, is on the left of the picture.

The poem beneath this print reads as follows:

All you that are curious downright
And fond of seeing every sight,
If to the Thames you had repaired
You might have seen a famous fair.
Diversions of every kind you'd see
With parties drinking of coffee and tea,
And dancing too I do declare
Upon the Thames they call Frost Fair.
It was really curious for to see
Both old and young so full of glee
The drinking booths they entered in
And call'd away for purl and Gin
Some played at Threadle my Needle Nan
The lasses slipt down as they ran
Which made the men quite full of glee
The young girls' legs for all to see.

The Watermen so neat and trim
With bottle filled with Old Tom's Gin
And others bawled among the throng
Who's for a glass of Sampson strong?
Here's nuts and gingerbread: who buys?
Come, boys, and win my mutton pies.
Come, ladies, they're both hot and nice;
Fear not to eat one on the ice.
Boys, men and women not a few
Upon the ice they ventured too
And swings there were I do declare
To take a ride up in the air
And booths wherein you might regale
And have a pint of beer or ale,
And skittle playing I do declare
Upon the Thames they call Frost Fair.

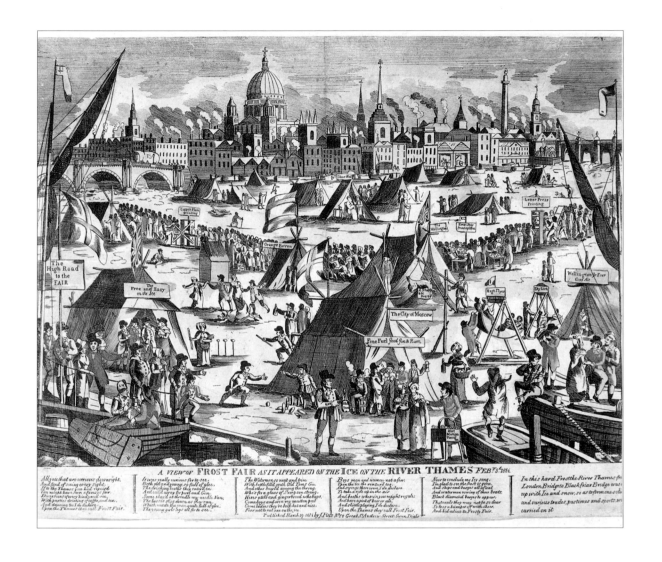

The print by J Pitts of Seven Dials.
This shows the most detail about this Fair,
and is reproduced at a larger scale on the next page.
Guildhall Library, Corporation of London

Those who took "The High Road to the Fair" found a cluster of taverns, from "The Free and Easy on the Ice", to "The City of Moscow", "The Wellington" and "Wellington for Ever". These last are a reminder of the political situation abroad: Wellington had been winning victories for Britain in the Peninsular war, and Napoleon had had to make his disastrous retreat from Moscow. Seen above one booth, the words Orange Boven, meaning "The orange are on top", refers to the fact that the French had also had to retreat from Holland, and the Dutch were back in charge.

In the foreground of the picture is a man selling hot mutton pies, the 18th century equivalent of mince-pies – indeed, mince pies still contain lard, the last remnant of the meat they used to contain. Next to the men playing the habitual ninepins, a group of men are drinking and smoking, under a sign reading "Fine Furl: Good Gin and Rum", though the man on the right clearly has a tankard of ale with a fine head to it.

In the middle distance, above the woman with her proto-coconut-shy, four people have joined hands, while a woman has slipped on the ice in front of them. As the poem underneath explains, "Some played at Threadle my Needle Nan, The Lassies slipt down as they ran, Which made the men quite full of glee, The young girls' legs for all to see."

"Threadle my Needle Nan" is possibly an early version of the children's game "In and Out the Windows", where children link hands and then wind through and under the arches created. Those words are sung to the tune of "The more we are together." (Another version is "In and Out the Dusty Bluebells", sung to the tune of "Bobby Shaftoe".) But a simpler game "Thread the Needle Dan" survived in children's playgrounds in Ireland at least until the 1950s.

Another view of the 1814 fair, with a sheep roasting vigorously above the fire. At left, below a banner proclaiming The King's Arms, a group of musicians play, sitting on a primitive stage of planks laid on the tops of barrels. In front of them, three couples dance to the music. A fancier bit of dancing is being produced by the young lady in the centre, who stands high above the multitude, walking on a tight-rope, or perhaps a wooden beam, while waving a flag of St. George in each hand.

One of a series of five slate panels, carved in about 1990, which are on show under the south end of Southwark Bridge. They are seen as one walks from London Bridge along the riverbank to visit the Globe.

However, parts of these carvings have been obscured by wooden platforms for over a year: let us hope the platforms are removed soon.

The Frost Fair of 1814, seen from the site of Southwark Bridge.
The line of stalls runs down the centre of the river, towards Old London Bridge.
At left, the tall warehouses of Three Cranes Wharf.
Guildhall Library, Corporation of London

From an engraving of 1600, showing the distinctive outline of the medieval St Paul's Cathedral, destroyed in 1666. The same outline appears in the painting shown overleaf.

Below the Cathedral, on the waterline can just be seen the three cranes, after which Three Cranes Wharf got its name.

Frost Fair on the Thames: before 1666

This fascinating glimpse of the frozen Thames was sold at Sothebys in April 1994 to an unknown private collector. An oil painting on panel by an unknown Dutchman, it must date from before 1666, as the outline of the medieval St Paul's appears as a silhouette on the right. This was destroyed in the Great Fire of London in 1666. On the left one can just see the rose window on the south side of Westminster Abbey. But the Abbey is hard to recognise, as it is shown without its two west towers, which were completed by Nicholas Hawksmoor in 1745.

As in 1739, the Thames had frozen at Westminster, and in the middle distance is a line of people walking across, past two booths erected on the ice. In the foreground is the only real sign of activity on the ice, with the usual ninepins, in this case, a line of tall wooden skittles, and a young man bowling at them.

The painting is almost more remarkable for the landscape it shows. Coming towards the viewer is a large embankment, with the river on the right and frozen marshland on the left. But it is the frozen marsh on the left which shows us Westminster still on its original island, Thorney Island, as it was called, surrounded by water. Indeed, the embankment is what we now call Millbank, so-called because the Abbot's millwheel used to run underneath it. So on the left now stand the major buildings of Millbank, including Tate Britain. This is possibly the only surviving view of the original Mill Bank.

A model of the frozen Thames, on show at the educational display next to the reconstructed Globe Theatre in Bankside. It is on permanent loan from the Museum of London.

The Frost Fairs: What can one see today?

Naturally, one would not expect anything to survive of the Frost Fairs themselves, apart from representations of them, and also the souvenirs printed on the ice. Copies of these souvenirs exist in several museums and libraries, including the Museum of London, which has the "royal" souvenir of 1684. Of the two paintings by Hondius in the Museum, the smaller one, of the Fair of 1683-4, is normally on view. (A copy of it is normally on show at Eltham Palace, near Greenwich.) The larger painting, of the Thames in 1677, takes so much more wall space to display, that it is only shown occasionally.

Jan Griffier's painting of the Frost Fair at Westminster in 1739 is normally on view in the lower gallery of the Guildhall Art Gallery, which contains the City of London's magnificent collection of historic paintings of London. The Gallery was recently rebuilt next to the Guildhall itself.

Apart from paintings, to get the best idea of the extent of these Fairs, one could take the Tube to Monument Station, then walk downhill to the riverside walk, and turn right, following the signs for the walk, until one comes to Southwark Bridge. Climb up to the Bridge, and start to walk across it on its eastern (downriver) side. Cannon Street Railway Bridge is on your left, and London Bridge visible through its piers. After a short time, look back to see the sign for Three Cranes Walk, on the riverbank down below, and then compare the modern view with the one shown earlier. As it happens, there is now an unusual high beam crane just to the east of Three Cranes Walk.

When you get close to the southern end of the Bridge, take the steps down to the lower level, and follow the path which leads towards the Globe. As you pass underneath Southwark Bridge, take the opportunity to look at the five slate panels showing the Frost Fairs. If you continue to the Globe, don't miss the model of the Frost Fair on show in the educational display beside the Globe.

If you turn in the opposite direction, to walk towards London Bridge, it is worth calling in at the new complex on the river side of Southwark Cathedral, which has an audio-visual display about early London, opened in 2001.

POSTSCRIPT: VIRGINIA WOOLF'S ORLANDO

In 1928, Virginia Woolf produced her novel "Orlando". It includes an evocative and magical description of a frost fair on the Thames in Tudor times. Indeed, many people know the fairs best through her description. But in it, she was using a novelist's imagination.

She portrays the fair as taking place next to Greenwich Palace, many miles downriver from London Bridge. The river did freeze at least once at this spot, as we are told that in 1537, "Jane Seymour, third Queen of Henry VIII, crossed the river on the ice to Greenwich Palace, on horseback, with the King." They were "attended by their whole court", so the ice supported a substantial weight on that occasion. But no frost fair took place there. Other details given in Orlando are also imaginary. For example, the ice is described as being "twenty fathoms deep". As a fathom measures six feet, the ice would thus have been 120 feet in depth – a great deal deeper than the river itself.

Virginia Woolf also describes a boat full of apples being visible at the bottom of the river, under the twenty fathoms of ice, and the woman who was selling the apples is also visible encased in the ice. All quite imaginary. The film version of Orlando includes some vivid scenes on the ice, and we see King James I looking at the apple boat through the ice – though this scene is only recognisable when one has read the passage in the novel.

Suffice to say that the novelist has conjured up a marvellous and evocative scene, but it is fictitious.

Somerset House, Christmas 2000

One of the best traces of the old Frost Fairs can be found in the quadrangle of Somerset House around Christmas time. After the parked cars, which filled the quadrangle, had been removed, it was reopened in the spring of 2000 with a permanent display of decorative water jets. But for Christmas that year, the quadrangle was turned into a skating rink, and this seems likely to be repeated every Christmas. Above is the quadrangle decorated for Christmas, while below are some of the skaters in December 2000.

The River's Tale, by Rudyard Kipling

Kipling wrote a splendid evocation of the history of the Thames, in a poem which is little known. It appeared in CLR Fletcher's "History of England" in 1911, and surely deserves to be as well known as "If".

Twenty bridges from Tower to Kew
(Twenty bridges or twenty two)
Wanted to know what the River knew,
For they were young and the Thames was old.
And this is the tale that the River told:

"I walk my beat before London Town
Five hours up and seven down.
Up I go till I end my run
At Tide-end-town, which is Teddington.
Down I come with the mud in my hands
And plaster it over the Maplin Sands.
But I'd have you know
that these waters of mine
Were once a branch of the River Rhine,
When hundreds of miles to the East I went
And England was joined to the Continent.

I remember the bat-winged lizard birds,
The Age of Ice and the mammoth herds,
And the giant tigers that stalked them down
Through Regent's Park into Camden Town.

And I remember like yesterday
The earliest Cockney who came my way,
When he pushed through the forest
that lined the Strand
With paint on his face and a club in his hand.

He was death to feather and fin and fur.
He trapped my beavers at Westminster.
He netted my salmon, he hunted my deer,
He killed my heron off Lambeth Pier.
He fought his neighbour with axes and swords,
Flint or bronze, at my upper fords,
While down at Greenwich, for slaves and tin,
The tall Phoenician ships stole in,
And North Sea war-boats, painted and gay,
Flashed like dragon-flies, Erith way;
And Norseman and Negro and Gaul and Greek
Drank with the Britons in Barking Creek.

And life was gay, and the world was new,
And I was a mile across at Kew!
But the Roman came with a heavy hand,
And bridged and roaded and ruled the land,
And the Roman left and the Danes blew in -
And that's where your history books begin!"

Nicholas Reed   *Portrait by Audrey Hammond, 2001*

THE AUTHOR

Nicholas Reed is a writer, publisher and photographer, and lectures for the National Association of Decorative and Fine Arts Societies and the National Trust. His most popular lecture, apart from the subject of the book, is "Artists' Views of the Thames through Five Centuries." Nicholas started as a Roman archaeologist, studying classics in Oxford, Manchester and St. Andrews. For the last fifteen years he has written on art history, specialising in the Impressionist painters of France and Britain.

He was Founder-Chairman of the Friends of Shakespeare's Globe, the Friends of West Norwood Cemetery, and the Edith Nesbit Society. He became Chairman of the Alliance of Literary Societies in 2001 and also edits the Newsletter of the Dulwich Society.

Audrey Hammond has been painting in Norwood for nearly forty years, and is perhaps best known for her book "Crystal Palace – Norwood Heights".

Further Reading

The only detailed review of the literary evidence for the Thames Frost Fairs was in "Famous Frosts and Frost Fairs" by W. Andrews, published in a limited edition in 1887.

"Frosts, Freezes and Fairs" by Ian Currie (1996) covers the whole of the British Isles from AD 1000, and includes the Thames.

For Old London Bridge, see "London Bridge", by Peter Jackson (Cassell, 1971). There has never been a detailed examination of the Thames Frost Fair pictures until now.

Acknowledgements

We are grateful to the Museum of London, the Guildhall Art Gallery and the Guildhall Library for permission to reproduce pictures in their possession. Other pictures reproduced are from the author's collection. In some cases we have not been able to trace the copyright owner.

Other books from Lilburne Press

Lilburne Press have produced a variety of historical and artistic books since 1989.

These include, by Nicholas Reed:

Monet and the Thames
Camille Pissarro at Crystal Palace
Pissarro in West London (Kew, Chiswick and Richmond)
Pissarro in Essex
Sisley and the Thames
Richmond and Kew: a souvenir guide
Whose Cat are You?: Forty Celebrities and their Cats

Among short illustrated biographies, they have published:

Edith Nesbit in SE London and Kent, by N. Reed
Enid Blyton in Beckenham and Bromley, by N. Reed
Arthur Conan Doyle, by Pat Moore
Richmal Crompton and her Bromley Connections, by Mary Cadogan